# Bedtime Stories
## for kids
### Short Funny Stories and Poems Collection for Children and Toddlers

**BUKKY EKINE-OGUNLANA**

© **Copyright** Bukky Ekine-Ogunlana 2025 – **All rights reserved.**

The content contained within this book may not be reproduced, duplicated, or transmitted without direct written permission from the author or the publisher.

Under no circumstance will any blame or legal responsibility be held against the publisher, or author, for any damages, reparation, or monetary loss due to the information contained within this book. Either directly or indirectly. You are responsible for your own choices, actions, and results.

Legal Notice:

This book is copyright protected. This book is only for personal use. You cannot amend, distribute, sell, use, quote, or paraphrase any part, or the content within this book, without the author or publisher's consent.

Disclaimer Notice:

Please note the information contained within this document is for educational and entertainment purposes only. All effort has been executed to present accurate, up-to-date, and reliable, complete information. No warranties of any kind are declared or implied. Readers acknowledge that the author is not engaging in the rendering of legal, financial, medical, or professional advice. The content within this book has been derived from various sources. Please consult a licensed professional before attempting any techniques outlined in this book

By reading this book, the reader agrees that under no circumstances is the author responsible for any losses, direct or indirect, which are incurred as a result of the use of the information contained within this document, including, but not limited to,—errors, omissions, or inaccuracies.

*Published by*

*TCEC Publishing*

*TCEC House*

*England, Great Britain.*

# Dedication

This lovely book is dedicated to all the beautiful students all over the world who, over the years, have passed through the T.C.E.C young adult's program. Thanks for the opportunity to serve you and invest in your colorful and bright future.

# Contents

Dedication ................................................................. 3

Introduction ............................................................. 7

Castle Trouble! ....................................................... 10

The Caterpillar's New Home ................................. 13

Stuck! ..................................................................... 16

The Patient Neighbour .......................................... 19

A Sorry Tale ........................................................... 22

The Lost Kite ......................................................... 25

The Brave Little Seed ........................................... 28

The Kindness Basket ............................................ 31

The Curious Little Star ......................................... 34

Benny's Big Balloon .............................................. 37

Lucy's Lost Locket ................................................ 40

The Rainbow Race ............................................... 43

The Gentle Giant .................................................. 46

The Little Lighthouse ........................................... 49

Timmy's Thank You .............................................. 51

Benny's Big Bubble .............................................. 53

Emma's Garden Helpers ...................................... 56

Max's Moonlight Adventure ................................ 58

Sophie's Smile .................................................................. 60

The Sharing Picnic ........................................................... 62

Leo's Lost Hat .................................................................. 64

Nora's Nightlight .............................................................. 66

Leave a Review! ............................................................... 69

Conclusion ........................................................................ 70

Other Books You'll Love! ................................................. 72

# Introduction

**The Beginning of a Meaningful Story Journey**

Dear Parent, Grandparent, or Loving Caregiver, Welcome to *Bedtime Stories for Kids*, the first joyful installment in the **Adventures in Faith & Healthy Living** series—a growing collection of heartwarming tales designed mainly to entertain, teach, and inspire young children.

In this first volume, your child will meet lovable characters and explore fun, relatable adventures—all while discovering essential life values like **honesty**, **gratitude**, **forgiveness**, and **teamwork**. These stories are written to delight and engage, turning powerful life lessons into playful, age-appropriate moments your child will remember.

Because these stories are often rooted in gentle morals and simple truths, they become more than just entertainment—they're stepping stones for learning. Rather than lecturing, these stories model behavior and values in a way that feels natural and exciting. Your child gets to giggle, wonder, and reflect—all at once.

## Why Stories Like These Matter

Children's stories have always held the power to teach without pressure. By reading stories like these aloud—or reading them together—you're helping your child:

- Expand vocabulary and early reading skills

- Recognize sounds, patterns, and sentence flow

- Grasp social-emotional learning through character actions

- Build focus, memory, and imagination

- Develop a healthy view of themselves and others

Shared reading is also one of the most loving things you can do. These stories create magical bonding time between you and your child. And when read aloud with warmth and enthusiasm, they teach values while encouraging **communication, confidence, and curiosity**.

If your child is just beginning to read, these tales offer repetition, rhyme, and rhythm that support literacy development. If they're listening, you can bring the characters to life with fun voices and sound effects—igniting their creativity while deepening their love for books.

Continue the Adventure!

We're thrilled to share that this is just the **first** of three connected storybooks designed with your child's growth in mind:

**Book 1**: *Bedtime Stories for Kids* (you're reading it now!)

**Book 2**: *More Adventures in Healthy Living* — continues with more fun tales focused on wellness, teamwork, kindness, and character

**Book 3**: *Faith & Fun Stories* — blends joyful storytelling with timeless faith-based values and gentle biblical themes

Each book builds on the last—helping your child explore deeper ideas through light-hearted, laugh-out-loud stories they'll want to revisit again and again.

So snuggle in close, flip the page, and prepare to explore a world where animals talk, trains work together, and even tiny acts of kindness can change everything.

Let the adventure begin!
With warmth,

The Adventures in Faith & Healthy Living Team
I would be incredibly thankful if you could take 60 seconds to write a brief review on the platform of purchase, even if it's just a few sentences!

# Castle Trouble!

A 3-Minute Funny Bedtime Tale with a Wise Builder Lesson

**Ages 3–8**

"Oh dear! Oh no!" cried Princess Amelie as raindrops thumped loudly on the old castle roof.

Drip-drop, splash-splosh! Water filled every corner—soon the walls had rivers running down them!

"My castle is crumbling!" she squealed, jumping from puddle to puddle. "It won't last another storm!"

She called for three fixers, who promised to repair the roof in three days.

Day one: They worked hard but only fixed a little.

Day two: They tried again, but the leaks kept coming.

"We'll never finish on time!" sighed one fixer, wiping sweat from his brow.

Then—rat-tat-tat!—a tiny fairy appeared with sparkling wings.

With a wave of her magic wand… ZING! The roof was brand new—solid and shiny!

The fairy smiled and whispered, "One good deed done!" before vanishing.

That night, Princess Amelie returned to a dry, shining castle and a magical party awaited—friends danced and laughed under the stars.

Princess Amelie smiled. "A strong foundation matters—whether for castles or for life!"

Giggle-Rhyme Wrap:
"Drip drop goes the rain,
Fixing magic ends the pain.
Builders small or builders tall,
With kind help, we can do it all!"

Moral:
A strong foundation matters—in castles and in life!

Bible Connection:
"Therefore everyone who hears these words of mine and puts them into practice is like a wise man who built his house on the rock."
— Matthew 7:24

Talk About It:
- What would you do if your roof was leaky?
- How can we build strong hearts like a strong castle?
- Who helps you when you need to fix something?

Activity Ideas:
- **Draw it!**: Draw Princess Amelie's shiny new castle.
- **Word Find:** Words to find — castle, rain, roof, fix, fairy, strong.
- **Mini-Challenge:** Build a "castle" with blocks or pillows at home.

Curriculum Tie-In:
- Science: Understand weather effects (rain and water damage).
- Social-emotional: Perseverance, asking for help.
- Faith: Understanding Jesus as the solid "rock" we build on.

# The End

# The Caterpillar's New Home

**Age Range:** 3–7 years

**Theme:** Honesty, Forgiveness, Teamwork

Deep in the green forest, a busy little caterpillar was tired of sleeping on slippery leaves.

"I'm going to build a leafy house—with walls and everything!" he declared.

He stitched leaves and sticks, hammered twigs, and stacked moss until his new home stood tall.

"I'm done!" he smiled proudly and ran to show his friend Hedgehog.

But oh no! He had built the house right in the middle of the forest trail!

Along came Fox, whistling happily—then stopped short.

"There's a house here? Right on my path?"

Fox tiptoed carefully around it. Next came Stork, warning Platypus not to crush the house by accident.

Suddenly, Fox sneezed—"Ah... ah... AH-CHOO!"

CRASH! The leafy house exploded into sticks and leaves everywhere!

"Oh no!" Fox cried. "I blew it down!"

Stork told Fox to tell the truth, but Fox was scared.

When Caterpillar returned, Fox lied, blaming a human for the mess.

But Caterpillar knew the truth and said kindly, "It was an accident. Let's rebuild it—together."

They worked as a team and built a new house behind a big tree, safe from sneezes and paws.

Giggle-Rhyme Wrap:
"Leaves can fly and sticks can fall,
But friends who help are best of all.
Truth may wobble, but it won't fall flat—
Kindness always fixes that!"

Moral:
Honesty builds trust. Telling the truth and working together brings healing and friendship.

**Bible Verse:**
"Stop telling lies. Tell your neighbor the truth."
— Ephesians 4:25

**Talk About It:**
- Have you ever accidentally broken something? What did you do?
- Why is telling the truth important, even when it's hard?
- How can you help friends who make mistakes?

**Activity Ideas:**
- **Draw it:** Draw Caterpillar's new leafy house.
- **Word Search:** Words: truth, friend, build, forest, help.
- **Mini-Challenge:** Think of a time you told the truth — share it with someone.

**Curriculum Tie-In:**
- Social-emotional: Honesty, forgiveness, teamwork.
- Literacy: Story sequencing, new vocabulary.
- Faith: Biblical truth and forgiveness lessons.

# The End

# Stuck!

A Winter Train Adventure in Teamwork

**Age Range:** 3–7 years

**Theme:** Cooperation, Perseverance, Kindness

It was the heart of winter, and the little steam train chugged through snowy mountains.

Families snuggled inside, wrapped in blankets, ready for Christmas holidays.

Suddenly—CLATTER-CLUNK!—the train stopped by a snowy bridge.

Outside, huge snowdrifts blocked the tracks.

Passengers pressed their noses to frosty windows, wondering what would happen next.

"I know what to do!" said little Lucy, raising her hand.

"We can all dig the snow away!"

At first, Mr. Grump frowned, "That sounds like too much work."

But when shovels came out, Lucy rallied everyone.

Together, they pulled on gloves and scarves and began digging—one scoop at a time.

Mrs. Piper made hot cocoa and passed cups to warm the workers.

Some got tired and grumbled, but they kept going, cheering each other on.

Finally, the tracks were clear!

The train chugged back to life—CHOOGA-CHOOGA-WHEEE!

Everyone cheered, proud they had worked together.

## Mini-Poem Wrap:

Snow may pile and wheels may stick,
But helping hands make problems quick.
Side by side, we push and sing—
Together, we make courage spring!

## Moral:

Working together, even when it's hard, helps us overcome obstacles.

## Bible Verse:

"Two are better than one… for if one falls, the other will lift them up." — Ecclesiastes 4:9

**Talk About It:**
- Have you ever worked with friends to solve a problem?
- How can we be kind to friends who get tired?
- What can you do to help someone feeling cold or sad?

**Activity Ideas:**
- **Coloring Page:** The train stuck in snow.
- **Drawing Prompt:** Draw your own teamwork adventure.
- **Mini-Challenge:** Help your family with a task this week.

**Curriculum Tie-In:**
- Social skills: Cooperation, empathy and perseverance.
- Faith: Biblical teamwork and caring.
- Literacy: Sound words and sequencing.

# The End

# The Patient Neighbour

A Warm Tale of Kindness and Boundaries

**Age Range:** 3–7 years

**Theme:** Kindness, Patience, Healthy Boundaries

In a cheerful toy-town lived Billy, a kind but forgetful boy.

Every night, he knocked on his neighbor Harrison's door, asking for matches, then milk, then socks!

Harrison always smiled and said "Yes," but night after night, he grew more tired.

One evening, after a long day, Harrison sighed when Billy knocked again.

Though weary, Harrison gave him tea, snacks, and more matches.

The next night, Billy asked for socks. Harrison gave them, but he felt worn out.

On the third night, Harrison snapped, "Take all my socks—just please stop bothering me!"

Billy was shocked, and Harrison immediately regretted his words.

Later, Harrison realized he needed to set gentle boundaries to keep friendship healthy.

At bedtime, Billy looked at his lonely socks and felt sad—but remembered Harrison's kindness.

Mini-Poem Wrap:
Kindness shared is warm and bright,
But even kind hearts need their night.
Caring is good, but fair and clear,
Helps both friends stay calm and dear.

Moral:
It's good to help others—but it's also kind to set gentle boundaries.

Bible Verse:
"Carry each other's burdens..."
— Galatians 6:2

Talk About It:
- How could Billy help Harrison feel better?
- Why do we all need rest and time alone sometimes?

- How can you kindly say "not now" to a friend?

Activity Ideas:
- **Role-Play:** Practice asking for help and saying "not now."
- **Drawing:** Draw Billy and Harrison sharing tea.
- **Mini-Challenge:** Think of a time you needed a break—share with a grown-up.

Curriculum Tie-In:
- Social-emotional: Patience, boundaries and kindness.
- Faith: Loving service balanced with wisdom.
- Literacy: Narrative structure, dialogue practice.

# A Sorry Tale

A Lesson about Honesty and Friendship

**Age Range:** 3–7 years

**Theme:** Integrity, Apology, Forgiveness

At Forest School, the Weasels and Badgers competed in a foraging challenge.

Wilbur Weasel had a sneaky plan—he whispered, "Let's cheat!"

While Basil Badger was fetching berries, Wilbur gobbled up all of Basil's berries!

Basil was upset and tipped over Wilbur's basket in anger.

When Mr. Hare, the teacher, came to check, both baskets were empty.

Basil blamed Wilbur; Wilbur blamed Basil.

Mr. Hare said, "You both misbehaved. Time to make things right."

Wilbur said, "I'm sorry for cheating."

Basil said, "I'm sorry for getting angry."

They shook paws and promised to be honest friends.

Mini-Poem Wrap:
Words that lie may cause a fight,
But saying sorry feels just right.
True friends pause to make things fair,
And kindness heals when we all care.

Moral:
Honesty and kindness build strong friendships. Saying sorry heals.

Bible Verse:
"Whoever speaks the truth tells what is right."
— Proverbs 12:17

Talk About It:
- Why was cheating wrong?
- How do you think saying sorry help friends?
- When have you said sorry to someone?

Activity Ideas:
- **Story Retell:** Act out the story with friends or family.
- **Drawing:** Draw Wilbur and Basil shaking paws.

- **Mini-Challenge:** Practice saying "I'm sorry" this week.

Curriculum Tie-In:
- Social skills: Honesty, forgiveness, conflict resolution.
- Faith: Biblical integrity.
- Literacy: Dialogue and narrative understanding.

# The Lost Kite

A Windy Day Adventure About
Patience and Hope

**Age Range:** 3–7 years

**Theme:** Patience, Hope and Perseverance

One windy morning, Leo the little fox ran outside with his brand-new red kite.

"Today, I'll fly it higher than the clouds!" he cheered.

He ran and ran, letting the kite catch the wind. Up, up, up it soared—then suddenly, WHOOSH! The kite snapped free from the string!

"Oh no!" cried Leo as the kite tumbled into the tall trees by the river.

Leo scrambled under branches, looking for the kite's bright red tail.

"Maybe I can climb up!" he thought. But the tree was too tall and the branches too thin.

Just then, a wise old owl blinked down at Leo.

"Patience, little one," said Owl. "Some things take time. You can't rush the wind."

Leo sat down and waited, watching the wind dance in the leaves.

The next day, Leo returned with his friends, and together they found the kite caught in the bushes near the riverbank.

"Teamwork and patience win the day!" smiled Leo as they carefully pulled the kite free.

That afternoon, Leo's kite soared higher than ever, and he laughed as it danced in the breeze.

Mini-Poem Wrap:
"Winds may take our toys away,
But hope and patience save the day.
With friends to help and hearts so bright,
We'll catch the kite and hold on very tight!"

Moral:
Patience and hope help us overcome setbacks.

Bible Verse:
"Be joyful in hope, patient in affliction, faithful in prayer." — Romans 12:12

Talk About It:
- Have you ever lost something important? How did you feel?
- Why is patience important when things go wrong?
- How can friends help when you're upset?

Activity Ideas:
- **Draw It:** Draw Leo flying his kite high in the sky.
- **Word Search:** Words to find — kite, wind, tree, friends, patience.
- **Mini-Challenge:** Try to be patient when waiting today — tell someone about it.

Curriculum Tie-In:
- Social-emotional: Patience, teamwork, hope.
- Science: Wind and weather effects.
- Faith: Trust and perseverance.

# The Brave Little Seed

A Growing Story About Courage and Faith

**Age Range:** 3–7 years

**Theme:** Courage, Growth and Faith

One sunny morning, a tiny seed lay in the soft earth. "I'm so small," said the seed. "How can I ever grow big and very strong?"

But the warm sun smiled down and the gentle rain whispered, "Be brave. You are meant for great things."

Day by day, the seed pushed up through the soil. Sometimes the wind shook the earth, and sometimes little bugs nibbled the leaves.

"Don't give up!" the wind hummed. "Keep growing!"

With faith and courage, the seed grew into a tall, bright sunflower, turning its face toward the sun.

The animals of the meadow admired the brave little seed's journey—from tiny and scared to bold and shining.

Mini-Poem Wrap:
"From tiny seed to flower tall,
Brave hearts grow and never fall.
With faith and hope, we stretch and rise—
Sunshine smiles in our eyes!"

Moral:
Even the smallest beginnings can grow into something wonderful with courage and faith.

Bible Verse:
"Have faith in God," Jesus said. — Mark 11:22

Talk About It:
- Have you ever tried something new that scared you?
- How does having faith help us be brave?
- What can you do to grow like the seed?

Activity Ideas:
- **Plant a Seed:** Grow a seed in a cup and watch it grow!
- **Coloring:** A brave sunflower reaching for the sun.
- **Mini-Challenge:** Say a prayer for courage today.

Curriculum Tie-In:
- Science: Plant growth and life cycles.

- Social skills: Courage and perseverance.

- Faith: Trusting God's plan.

# The Kindness Basket

A Sweet Story About Sharing and Generosity

**Age Range:** 3–7 years

**Theme:** Kindness, Sharing and Generosity

In a busy village, Mia the mouse carried a big basket filled with fresh fruits and nuts.

"I want to share this with my friends," she said happily.

Mia went door to door, giving apples to the rabbits, nuts to the squirrels, and berries to the birds.

Each friend smiled and shared a warm "Thank you!"

But when Mia's basket was almost empty, she found a little kitten shivering outside.

"Oh no! I have almost nothing left," Mia worried.

The kitten looked up with big eyes. "It's okay. Sharing makes you happy, even when you have little."

Mia smiled and gave the kitten the last apple.

That day, everyone in the village felt a little brighter, thanks to Mia's kindness basket.

**Mini-Poem Wrap:**
"Kindness grows when we share,
Even if there's little to spare.
A giving heart is full and sweet—
Helping others is a treat!"

**Moral:**
Generosity and kindness make the world a happier place.

**Bible Verse:**
"Share with the Lord's people who are in need."
— Romans 12:13

**Talk About It:**
- What's something that is kind you've done recently?
- How does sharing make you feel?
- Why is it important to help others?

**Activity Ideas:**
- **Draw a Kindness Basket:** Fill it with things you would share.
- **Word Scramble:** kindness, share, friends, basket.
- **Mini-Challenge:** Do a kind deed for someone today.

Curriculum Tie-In:
- Social-emotional: Empathy and generosity.
- Faith: Biblical teaching on giving.
- Literacy: Vocabulary building with kindness words.

# The Curious Little Star

A Nighttime Tale About Wonder and Trust

**Age Range:** 3–7 years

**Theme:** Curiosity, Trust and Wonder

Every night, little Star twinkled high in the sky.

"I want to know everything about the world below!" she wondered.

One night, Star asked the Moon, "How do you shine so bright?"

The Moon smiled softly. "Because I trust the sun to warm me during the day."

Star blinked and thought, "Maybe I can trust too."

From that night on, Star shone with a calm, steady light, lighting the way for sleepy children and wandering animals.

She learned that sometimes, trusting and waiting is the best way to shine.

Mini-Poem Wrap:
"Curious eyes that shine so bright,
Trust and wait for morning light.
Wonder grows when hearts believe—
Magic happens when we receive."

Moral:
Trusting in God's timing helps us shine in our own way.

Bible Verse:
"Trust in the Lord with all your heart."
— Proverbs 3:5

Talk About It:
- What are you curious about?
- How can trust help you feel calm?
- When do you feel like shining your brightest?

Activity Ideas:
- **Star Craft:** Make a twinkling star from paper and glitter.
- **Drawing Prompt:** Draw what you see when you look at the night sky.

- **Mini-Challenge:** Share one wonder that you saw today with a friend.

Curriculum Tie-In:
- Science: Night sky and stars.
- Emotional learning: Trust and patience.
- Faith: Trusting God's plan.

# Benny's Big Balloon

A Fun Flight Story About Courage and Letting Go

**Age Range:** 3–7 years

**Theme:** Courage, Letting Go, Joy

Benny the bear had a bright yellow balloon.

"I'll take it to the very top of the hill!" he said.

Up the hill Benny ran, holding the string tight. But suddenly, a gust of wind tugged the balloon free!

"Oh no!" Benny shouted as the balloon soared away.

Benny felt sad but then remembered what Grandma Bear told him: "Sometimes we have to let go to see new things."

So Benny smiled, watching his balloon fly across the sky.

He ran down the hill, ready for a new adventure—because sometimes courage means saying goodbye.

Mini-Poem Wrap:

"Sometimes we hold, sometimes we let go,
Brave hearts grow more than we know.
Joy is found in every flight—
New adventures shine so bright!"

Moral:

Courage means accepting change and looking forward to new joys.

Bible Verse:

"Be strong and courageous." — Joshua 1:9

Talk About It:

- What is something that you have had to let go of?
- How can being brave help when things change?
- What new adventures are you excited about?

Activity Ideas:

- **Balloon Drawing:** Draw Benny and his balloon flying high.
- **Coloring Page:** A hill with balloons floating in the sky.
- **Mini-Challenge:** Try something new today!

Curriculum Tie-In:

- Emotional learning: Coping with change and courage.

- Faith: Biblical courage stories.

- Literacy: Simple narrative with exciting action.

# Lucy's Lost Locket

A Gentle Story About Honesty and Help

**Age Range:** 3–7 years

**Theme:** Honesty, Friendship and Helpfulness

Lucy the lamb loved her shiny silver locket. It was a gift from her grandmother.

One sunny day, Lucy noticed her locket was missing!

"Oh no! Where could it be?" she fretted.

She looked under bushes, behind trees, and even asked her friends.

Her friend Freddy the fox found the locket near the pond.

"Is this yours?" Freddy asked.

Lucy smiled, "Thank you for telling the truth!"

Together, they cleaned the locket and hung it safely around Lucy's neck.

Lucy learned that honesty and helping friends makes troubles smaller.

Mini-Poem Wrap:

"Lost things found and friends so true,

Honesty helps you and me.

Helping hands and hearts so bright,

Make the day feel warm and light."

Moral:

Trust is built when you are honest with people.

Bible Verse:

"Each one should speak the truth."

— Ephesians 4:25

Talk About It:

- Have you ever lost something? What did you do?
- Why is telling the truth important?
- Who can you ask for help when you need it?

Activity Ideas:

- **Lost and Found Game:** Hide small items and find them with a friend.

- **Drawing:** Picture of Lucy and Freddy with the locket.

- **Mini-Challenge:** Tell the truth even if it's hard.

Curriculum Tie-In:
- Social skills: Honesty and trust.

- Literacy: Narrative and dialogue.

- Faith: Biblical truthfulness.

# The Rainbow Race

A Colorful Story About Fairness and Fun

**Age Range:** 3–7 years

**Theme:** Fairness, Sportsmanship and Joy

One bright morning, animals gathered for the Rainbow Race.

Red fox, yellow canary, blue bunny, and green turtle lined up at the start.

"Ready... set... GO!" called the owl.

Everyone ran as fast as they could.

Blue bunny sped ahead, but saw green turtle moving slowly.

"I'll wait for you!" said blue bunny with a smile.

Red fox and yellow canary cheered.

Together, they crossed the finish line—side by side!

The prize? Friendship and fun!

Mini-Poem Wrap:
>"Run and jump, have fun and play,
>Fairness wins at the end of the day.
>Friends together, hand in hand,
>Joy is the best prize in the land!"

Moral:
Fairness and kindness make any game fun for everyone.

Bible Verse:
"Do to others as you would have them do to you." — Luke 6:31

Talk About It:
- What does fairness mean to you?
- How can you be a good friend during games?
- Why do you think having fun matters more than who wins?

Activity Ideas:
- **Coloring:** Animals that are racing with rainbow colors.
- **Game:** Organize a simple race and practice cheering friends.
- **Mini-Challenge:** Say "Good job!" to a friend today.

Curriculum Tie-In:
- Social-emotional: Sportsmanship and fairness.
- Faith: Treating others kindly.
- Physical activity: Movement and coordination.

# The Gentle Giant

A Heartwarming Tale About Kindness and Respect

**Age Range:** 3–7 years

**Theme:** Kindness, Respect, Understanding

In the valley lived George, the gentle giant. Though big and strong, George was shy and kind.

One day, the little animals were scared of George's loud footsteps.

"I don't want to scare them," George worried.

So George decided to show kindness instead.

He helped carry heavy logs, picked fruit for the birds, and gently rocked baby bunnies to sleep.

Slowly, the animals saw George's gentle heart—and loved him dearly.

Mini-Poem Wrap:
"Big or small, soft or loud,
Kindness makes us all so proud.

Gentle hearts can always shine—
Friendship grows with love divine."

**Moral:**
Kindness and respect help us understand and appreciate others.

**Bible Verse:**
> "Be kind and compassionate to one another."
> — Ephesians 4:32

**Talk About It:**
- In what ways can you show that you are kind to others around you?
- Why is it important to respect everyone?
- Have you ever been shy like George? What helped you?

**Activity Ideas:**
- **Role-play:** Practice kind words and actions.
- **Drawing:** George helping the animals.
- **Mini-Challenge:** Do something kind for someone today.

Curriculum Tie-In:
- Social skills: Empathy and respect.

- Faith: Biblical kindness.

- Literacy: Simple story with dialogue.

# The Little Lighthouse

A Bright Story About Guidance and Hope

**Age Range:** 3–7 years

**Theme:** Guidance, Hope and Faith

On a rocky shore stood a little lighthouse. Every night, it shone its light to guide ships safely home. One stormy night, the light flickered and went out!

"Oh no! The ships will crash!" worried the lighthouse keeper.

But a small boy climbed the tower and fixed the lamp.

The light shone bright again, and the ships sailed safely.

The little lighthouse learned that even when scared, help and hope can light the way.

Mini-Poem Wrap:
"Shining bright through storm and night,
Guiding ships with hopeful light.

When we help and show we care,
Hope and love are everywhere."

**Moral:**
Faith and helping others guide us through dark times.

**Bible Verse:**
"Your word is a lamp to my feet."
— Psalm 119:105

**Talk About It:**
- Who helps guide you when you feel scared?
- How can you be a light for others?
- What does hope mean to you?

**Activity Ideas:**
- **Craft:** Make a paper lighthouse with light.
- **Drawing:** Stormy sea with shining lighthouse.
- **Mini-Challenge:** Find someone around you, who is very scared and help that person out today.

**Curriculum Tie-In:**
- Science: Light and safety.
- Emotional learning: Hope and courage.
- Faith: God's guidance.

# Timmy's Thank You

A Heartfelt Story About Gratitude

**Age Range:** 3–7 years

**Theme:** Gratitude, Appreciation, Joy

Timmy the turtle loved his garden. One day, a big storm knocked down his favorite flower. "I'm sad," Timmy sighed.

But his friends brought new seeds, watering cans, and smiles.

"Thank you!" Timmy said, feeling happy and loved.

He learned that saying thank you makes joy grow big.

Mini-Poem Wrap:
"Thank you, thank you, loud and clear,
Grateful hearts bring lots of cheer.
Friends and kindness, love so true,
Joy grows more when we say 'Thank you!'"

Moral:

Gratitude helps us see the good in every day and in every friend that we have.

Bible Verse:

"Give thanks to the Lord, for he is good."
— Psalm 107:1

Talk About It:
- What are you thankful for today?
- How do you say thank you?
- Why is gratitude important?

Activity Ideas:
- **Thank You Cards:** Make cards for family or friends.
- **Drawing:** Timmy's garden blooming with flowers.
- **Mini-Challenge:** Say thank you three times today.

Curriculum Tie-In:
- Social skills: Gratitude and appreciation.
- Faith: Thankfulness to God.
- Literacy: Expressing feelings in words.

# Benny's Big Bubble

---

A Fun Story About Patience and Sharing

**Age Range:** 3–7 years

**Theme:** Patience, Sharing and Fun

Benny the bunny loved blowing big bubbles that are fun. One windy day, he tried to make the biggest bubble ever! Pop! It burst too soon.

"Oh no!" Benny frowned.

His friend Mia said, "Try again, Benny! I'll help you."

They took turns blowing bubbles, sharing the bubble wand.

Slowly, Benny learned to be patient—and the bubbles grew bigger and bigger!

**Mini-Poem Wrap:**
"Blow a bubble, big and bright,
Patience helps it take its flight.
Sharing fun with friends so near,
Makes the day full of cheer!"

**Moral:**
Patience and sharing make fun last longer and feel better.

**Bible Verse:**
"Be patient, bearing with one another in love."
— Ephesians 4:2

**Talk About It:**
- What does patience mean?
- How do you feel when someone shares with you?
- Can you think of a time you waited for something?

**Activity Ideas:**
- **Bubble blowing:** Practice blowing bubbles together.
- **Drawing:** Benny and Mia with big bubbles.
- **Mini-Challenge:** Share a toy or game today.

Curriculum Tie-In:
- Social skills: Patience and sharing.

- Science: How bubbles form.

- Faith: Loving kindness.

# Emma's Garden Helpers

A Helpful Story About Cooperation and Growth

**Age Range:** 3–7 years

**Theme:** Cooperation, Helping, Growth

Emma planted seeds in her garden. But the weeds started to grow fast! "Oh no, my flowers!" Emma cried.

Her friends came to help—pulling weeds, watering, and planting new seeds.

Together, they worked happily, and soon colorful flowers bloomed everywhere!

Mini-Poem Wrap:
"Working together, side by side,
Helping hands make gardens very wide.
Friends can grow and bloom with cheer,
When we help each other here!"

## Moral:
Working together helps everyone grow and succeed.

## Bible Verse:
"Two are better than one." — Ecclesiastes 4:9

## Talk About It:
- How can you help others?
- Why is teamwork important?
- What do you like to plant or grow?

## Activity Ideas:
- **Planting seeds:** Try planting something at home or school.
- **Drawing:** Draw yourself and your friend working in the garden.
- **Mini-Challenge:** Help someone with a task today.

## Curriculum Tie-In:
- Science: Plant growth.
- Social: Cooperation skills.
- Faith: Helping others.

# Max's Moonlight Adventure

A Nighttime Story About Courage and Faith

**Age Range:** 3–7 years

**Theme:** Courage, Faith and Exploration

Max the mouse was afraid of the dark.
One night, the full moon shone bright.
Max decided to explore the garden by moonlight.

At first, he shivered, but he remembered God's promise to always be near.

With courage, Max found sparkling fireflies and soft night flowers.

He wasn't afraid anymore!

Mini-Poem Wrap:
"Moonlight glows and stars so bright,
God's love shines through out the night.
With courage that is strong, I dare to see,

The wonders that can come to me."

## Moral:
Faith gives us courage to face what scares us.

## Bible Verse:
> "Even though I walk through the darkest valley,
> I will fear no evil." — Psalm 23:4

## Talk About It:
- What scares you sometimes?
- How can faith help you feel brave?
- What do you like about nighttime?

## Activity Ideas:
- **Night drawing:** Stars, moon, and fireflies.
- **Story time:** Share your own courage stories.
- **Mini-Challenge:** Try doing one brave thing today.

## Curriculum Tie-In:
- Emotional: Managing fear.
- Faith: Trust in God.
- Science: Nighttime animals and stars.

# Sophie's Smile

A Bright Story About Kindness and Sharing Joy

**Age Range:** 3–7 years

**Theme:** Kindness, Joy, Friendship

Sophie loved to smile.

One rainy day, her friends felt sad.

Sophie smiled at each friend, and soon smiles spread all around.

"Your smile makes me happy!" said her friend Leo.

Sophie learned that sharing joy is the best gift of all.

Mini-Poem Wrap:

"A smile can light a cloudy day,
Chasing all the gloom away.
Share your smile, make friends so bright,
Joy grows stronger with each light."

Moral:

Kindness and smiles brighten everyone's day.

**Bible Verse:**
> "A cheerful heart is good medicine."
> — Proverbs 17:22

**Talk About It:**
- What makes you want to smile to people?
- How do you think your smile can make someone else feel?
- Can you find a moment to share your smile with someone today?

**Activity Ideas:**
- **Smile drawing:** Make happy faces.
- **Game:** Smile at friends and see who smiles back.
- **Mini-Challenge :** Give someone a smile today.

**Curriculum Tie-In:**
- Social: Friendship and Kindness .
- Emotional: Happiness and joy.
- Faith: Joy from God.

# The Sharing Picnic

**A Sweet Story About Generosity and Friendship**

**Age Range:** 3–7 years

**Theme:** Generosity, Friendship, Sharing

The animals planned a picnic.

Everyone brought their favorite food to share.

At the picnic, the food was spread out, and friends tried new treats.

"Thank you for sharing!" said Bella the bear.

Sharing made the picnic delicious and fun!

Mini-Poem Wrap:

"Sharing food and friends so dear,
Makes our hearts feel full of cheer.
Give a little, give a lot,
Sharing love means happy spots!"

Moral:

Sharing with friends brings happiness to everyone.

**Bible Verse:**
> "Share with the Lord's people who are in need."
> — Romans 12:13

**Talk About It:**
- What is your favorite food to share?
- How do you feel when someone shares with you?
- Why is sharing important?

**Activity Ideas:**
- **Picnic pretend play:** Share snacks with friends or family.
- **Drawing:** Picnic with animals sharing food.
- **Mini-Challenge:** Share something with a friend today.

**Curriculum Tie-In:**
- Social skills: Generosity and sharing.
- Faith: Giving and kindness.
- Practical: Healthy eating and food sharing.

# Leo's Lost Hat

A Gentle Tale About Honesty and Help

**Age Range:** 3–7 years

**Theme:** Honesty, Asking for Help and Friendship

Leo the lion loved his bright red hat.
One windy day, the hat flew off and disappeared!
Leo looked everywhere, but couldn't find it.

He felt sad but decided to ask his friends for help.

Together, they two of them searched the tall grass, under bushes, and behind rocks.

At last, Mia the mouse spotted the hat on a tree branch.

Leo smiled, "Thank you for helping me find my hat!"

Mini-Poem Wrap:
"When things get lost and can't be found,
Ask for help, look all around.
Friends will help with an open heart,
Honesty is a great place to start!"

**Moral:**

Being honest and asking for help brings friends closer together and helps solve problems.

**Bible Verse:**

"Therefore, encourage one another and build each other up."
— 1 Thessalonians 5:11

**Talk About It:**
- Have you ever lost something?
- Who do you ask when you need help?
- Why is it good to be honest?

**Activity Ideas:**
- **Hide and seek:** Hide an object and find it together.
- **Drawing:** Leo and friends searching for the hat.
- **Mini-Challenge:** Help a friend today.

**Curriculum Tie-In:**
- Social: Asking for help, teamwork.
- Emotional: Dealing with loss.
- Faith: Encouragement and honesty.

# Nora's Nightlight

A Cosy Story About Trust and Comfort

**Age Range:** 3–7 years

**Theme:** Trust, Comfort and God's Presence

Nora was afraid of the dark.
She asked her mom for a nightlight.
But one night, the light bulb burned out!

Nora felt scared again.

Her mom cuddled her close and said, "God's light is always with you, even in the dark."

Nora closed her eyes and felt a wave of calm wash over her, knowing that God was with her.

She whispered, "Thank you, God."

**Mini-Poem Wrap:**

"When the night is dark and deep,

God's love is mine to keep.

Close your eyes, there is no need to fear,

His light is always near."

**Moral:**

God's love is a constant, unwavering light that never goes out and always there to comfort us even in the darkest times.

**Bible Verse:**

"The Lord is my light and my salvation—whom shall I fear?"

— Psalm 27:1

**Talk About It:**
- What makes you feel scared?
- How can you remember God's love?
- What comforts you at night?

**Activity Ideas:**
- **Craft:** Make a paper nightlight.
- **Story time:** Share favourite comfort objects.
- **Mini-Challenge:** Say a prayer before bed.

Curriculum Tie-In:
- Emotional: Managing fear.

- Faith: God's protection and love.

- Practical: Bedtime routines.

# Leave a Review!

I hope you have enjoyed these stories. I would be incredibly thankful if you could take 60 seconds to write a brief review on the platform of purchase, even if it's just a few sentences!

# Conclusion

Keep Reading, Keep Growing

When it comes to giving your kids a head start, reading books together is one of the most powerful tools you can use. It sparks imagination, builds confidence, strengthens vocabulary, and—most importantly—nurtures emotional intelligence and moral development. These simple bedtime tales are more than just fun—they're little blueprints for how to be kind, honest, brave, and thoughtful in everyday life.

The stories in this book present easy-to-understand lessons on topics like gratitude, teamwork, and forgiveness—values that are essential in early childhood. And because these lessons are presented through laughter, rhyme, and lovable characters, your child will absorb important truths **without even realizing they're learning**.

Shared reading also builds strong habits for school success. A child who regularly listens to or reads stories is more likely to enter school with a solid grasp of phonics, vocabulary, and comprehension. It also improves listening skills, creativity, and emotional bonding between you and your little one.

Some children may even be inspired to act out these tales as mini plays or puppet shows—another fantastic way to build communication skills, creative confidence, and expressive language. Whether you're reading aloud, using silly voices, or letting your child retell the story in their own words, these bedtime moments are laying the foundation for a lifelong love of reading.

## Ready for More?

If you and your child enjoyed this book, we invite you to continue your journey with us! *Bedtime Stories for Kids* is just the **first** book in the **Adventures in Faith & Healthy Living** series.

**Book 2: *More Adventures in Healthy Living*** — dive into another round of uplifting, funny, and heart-smart tales about wellness, good choices, and growing strong in body and character.

**Book 3: *Faith & Fun Stories*** — take your child deeper into meaningful values rooted in simple biblical truths, with joyful faith-based stories that encourage kindness, courage, and spiritual growth.

Each book is crafted to stand alone—but together, they form a treasure trove of learning, laughter, and love.

So don't stop here—snuggle up for Book 2 next!

Let's keep reading, keep imagining, and keep growing... together.

With encouragement and joy,
**The Adventures in Faith & Healthy Living Team**

# Other Books You'll Love!

1. <u>The Fear of The Lord: How God's Honour Guarantees Your Peace</u>

2. Parenting Teenage Girls for Purpose: Guiding Godly Young Girls to Walk in Charisma, Character, Calling, Life Skills, and Christ-Centered Confidence

3. Parenting Teenage Boys for Purpose: Guiding Godly Young Girls to Walk in Charisma, Character, Calling, Life Skills, and Christ-Centered Confidence

4. <u>Raising Teenagers to Choose Wisely: Keeping your Teen Secure in a Big World</u>

5. <u>Spelling one: An Interactive Vocabulary & Spelling Workbook for 5-Year-Olds. *(With Audiobook Lessons)*</u>

6. <u>Spelling Two: An Interactive Vocabulary & Spelling Workbook for 6-Year-Olds. *(With Audiobook Lessons)*</u>

7. <u>Spelling Three: An Interactive Vocabulary & Spelling Workbook for 7-Year-Olds.</u> *<u>(With Audiobook Lessons)</u>*

8. <u>Spelling Four: An Interactive Vocabulary & Spelling Workbook for 8-Year-Olds.</u> *<u>(With Audiobook Lessons)</u>*

9. <u>Spelling Five: An Interactive Vocabulary & Spelling Workbook for 9-Year-Olds.</u> *<u>(With Audiobook Lessons)</u>*

10. <u>Spelling Six: An Interactive Vocabulary & Spelling Workbook for 10 & 11 Years Old.</u> *<u>(With Audiobook Lessons)</u>*

11. <u>Spelling Seven: An Interactive Vocabulary & Spelling Workbook for 12-14 Years-Old.</u> *<u>(With Audiobook Lessons)</u>*

12. <u>Raising Boys in Today's Digital World: Proven Positive Parenting Tips for Raising Respectful, Successful, and Confident Boys</u>

13. <u>Raising Girls in Today's Digital World: Proven Positive Parenting Tips for Raising Respectful, Successful, and Confident Girls</u>

14. <u>Raising Kids in Today's Digital World: Proven Positive Parenting Tips for Raising Respectful, Successful, and Confident Kids</u>

15. <u>The Child Development and Positive Parenting Master Class 2-in-1 Bundle: Proven Methods for Raising Well-</u>

Behaved and Intelligent Children, with Accelerated Learning Methods

16. Parenting Teens in Today's Challenging World 2-in-1 Bundle: Proven Methods for Improving Teenager's Behaviour with Positive Parenting and Family Communication

17. Life Strategies for Teenagers: Positive Parenting, Tips and Understanding Teens for Better Communication and a Happy Family

18. Parenting Teen Girls in Today's Challenging World: Proven Methods for Improving Teenager's Behaviour with Whole Brain Training

19. Parenting Teen Boys in Today's Challenging World: Proven Methods for Improving Teenager's Behaviour with Whole Brain Training

20. 101 Tips For Helping With Your Child's Learning: Proven Strategies for Accelerated Learning and Raising Smart Children Using Positive Parenting Skills

21. 101 Tips for Child Development: Proven Methods for Raising Children and Improving Kids Behavior with Whole Brain Training

22. Financial Tips to Help Kids: Proven Methods for Teaching Kids Money Management and Financial Responsibility

23. Healthy Habits for Kids: Positive Parenting Tips for Fun Kids Exercises, Healthy Snacks, and Improved Kids Nutrition

24. Mini Habits for Happy Kids: Proven Parenting Tips for Positive Discipline and Improving Kids' Behavior

25. Good Habits for Healthy Kids 2-in-1 Combo Pack: Proven Positive Parenting Tips for Improving Kid's Fitness and Children's Behavior

26. T Raising Teenagers to Choose Wisely: Keeping your Teen Secure in a Big World

27. Tips for #CollegeLife: Powerful College Advice for Excelling as a College Freshman

28. The Career Success Formula: Proven Career Development Advice and Finding Rewarding Employment for Young Adults and College Graduates

29. The Motivated Young Adult's Guide to Career Success and Adulthood: Proven Tips for Becoming a Mature Adult, Starting a Rewarding Career, and Finding Life Balance

30. Bedtime Stories for Kids: Short Funny Stories and poems Collection for Children and Toddlers

31. Guide for Boarding School Life

# Your Free Gift!

As a way of saying thank you for Your purchase, I have included a gift that you can download at TCEC publishing .com

www.ingramcontent.com/pod-product-compliance
Lightning Source LLC
Chambersburg PA
CBHW071540080526
44588CB00011B/1733